Dear
Some images of New
Zealand for you.
love
Daryl.

EXPLORE DREAM DISCOVER

a new zealand photographic journey

Jeff Drewitz

north island

northland 13
central north island 19
lower north island 35

south island

nelson & marlborough 45
west coast 51
canterbury 57
otago 65
fiordland & southland 75

The Champagne Pool hot spring, Wai-O-Tapu Thermal Wonderland, Rotorua.

The Moeraki Boulders, Otago.

Tasman Valley, Mt Cook/Aoraki National Park.

Clockwise from top left: – Hiking in Mt Cook National Park, South Island. – Surfer at Raglan. – Silver fern. – Yellow-eyed penguin. – 600 year-old kauri trees, Coromandel Peninsula. – Fur seal at Cape Palliser. – Campervan at sunset on Lake Pukaki. – Swan and coot on Lake Tekapo. – Kiwi. – Blue waters of Lake Pukaki.

In my travels around New Zealand, I heard more than a few visitors encouraged to skip the North Island in favour of the South Island and its spectacular scenery. Yet many of my favourite locations are on the North Island, which offers a wide variety of breathtaking sights. There's the secluded and mild Northland with the blue waters of the Bay of Islands, remote Cape Reinga and the brooding forests of the Kauri Coast. The amazing volcanic landscapes around Rotorua and the Tongariro Crossing provided, without a doubt, one of the best day walks I have ever done. Further to the south, there is Cape Palliser with fur seals on the rocky beach below the lighthouse. The North Island might hold less 'wilderness' than the south, but it holds a drama and majesty that is all its own. The North Island is a vital part of any trip to New Zealand.

◀ *Clockwise from top left: Sunrise, Bay of Plenty. – The Champagne Pool hot spring, Rotorua. – View from Te Mata Peak near sunset, Havelock North. – Cable car in Wellington. – Mt Ruapehu from the Mangatepopo Valley, Tongariro National Park. – Hahei Beach, Coromandel Peninsula.*

◀◀ *Golden sunrise light on the hills behind Cape Palliser, South Wairarapa.*

Northland

One of my favourite memories of travelling in New Zealand was doing the long drive up the dusty road to Cape Reinga. We got there at the end of the day, just in time to get a few shots of the lighthouse in the last of the day's light. I also have fond memories of staying the night next to Lake Taharoa and having the entire campsite to myself. I woke up early the next day to take the photo displayed to the left. For a photographer, it doesn't get much better than that!

Cape Reinga Lighthouse, near the northernmost point of the North Island.

Calm waters of Lake Taharoa in the morning, Kai Iwi Lakes.

Tall ship Soren Larsen under sail in the Bay of Islands.

Blue waters of the Bay of Islands from Urupukapuka Island.
Sweeping headland of Cape Maria van Diemen near the
Cape Reinga Lighthouse.

17

Central North Island

Despite being a city of 1.5 million, the Auckland region offers many great outdoor activities. You can take the ferry to islands such as Rangitoto for bushland hikes and to an endangered bird sanctuary on Tiritiri Matangi Island. The Waitakere Ranges Regional Park west of the city hosts some scenic waterfalls near Piha Beach including Kitekite Falls. But if you want to feel like you have most of the North Island to yourself, take a drive around East Cape. Pass the dramatically situated Raukokore Church and finish with a steep hike up to the East Cape Lighthouse. Despite the pervasive spoiled egg smell, the various bubbling mineral springs and geysers around Rotorua are well worth checking out, as are the brilliant sulphur pools of Tongariro National Park. To the south, dramatic Te Mata Peak rises 400m above Havelock North, providing great sunset and sunrise views.

The Auckland cityscape at dusk.

Golden light of a summer sunset on the rugged cliffs near Piha Beach.

Auckland Harbour Bridge.

Kitekite Falls in the Waitakere Ranges Regional Reserve, west of Auckland.

Gannets on Wainui Beach, near Auckland.

◁ The beautiful rock formation at Cathedral Cove.

23

Raukokore Church, Raukokore, East Cape.

◁ *Morning clouds on Mt Karioi, near Raglan.*

Marokopa Falls, west of Waitomo Caves.

The Emerald Lakes, Tongariro National Park.

27

Prince of Wales geyser, Rotorua.

← *The Champagne Pool hot spring,*
Wai-O-Tapu Thermal Wonderland, Rotorua.

Bridal Veil Falls, between Raglan and Kawhia.

◁ *Dramatic and secluded East Cape.*

*Clouds over the Tongariro
Plateau, Mangatepopo Valley,
Tongariro National Park.*

This area holds some of my most memorable New Zealand moments. I remember, quite clearly, stumbling out of my campervan at dawn at Cape Palliser and nearly standing on a sleeping fur seal. It was a surreal experience to get that close to nature while trying to get photos of the sunrise light. I remember waiting for the dawn light to fall on the cliffs next to Castlepoint Lighthouse, getting that misty look on the sea while the lighthouse light was still shining.

Mt Taranaki at sunset, viewed from Tongariro National Park.

Dawn at the Castlepoint Lighthouse, South Wairarapa.

Fog amongst the eerily eroded Putangirua
Pinnacles, South Wairarapa. ⟩

⟨ Fog at sunset, Te Mata Peak, Havelock North.

Wellington Cable Car, Wellington.

4 *Cape Palliser at sunrise.*

south island

For sheer variety of landscape, rugged beauty and wilderness, the South Island is hard – if not impossible – to beat. You can experience a multitude of natural spendours from a kayak trip in the clear blue waters off Abel Tasman National Park to the stormy waters of Curio Bay in the Catlins. You can take advantage of adventure activities from a helicopter trip over the glaciers and around the summit of Mount Cook to a gruelling hike up to French Ridge Hut in Mount Aspiring National Park. Whatever you do, there is an almost unending variety of breathtaking natural beauty to be found throughout the South Island.

◀ *Clockwise from top left: – Marlborough Sounds. – Sea kayaking at the Tonga Arches, Abel Tasman National Park. – Trampers crossing bridge in West Matukituki River valley, Mt Aspiring National Park. – Church of the Good Shepherd on the shore of Lake Tekapo. – Titirangi Bay, Marlborough Sounds. – Whataroa River near Whataroa, West Coast.*
◀◀ *Rainbow at sunset over Lake Pukaki.*

Nelson & Marlborough

As an introduction to the South Island following a ferry trip across the Cook Strait, Nelson and Marlborough don't disappoint. A rugged hike up the 1,200m Mount Stokes through moss-covered rainforest opens out into a spectacular view over the Marlborough Sounds. A 20-minute walk over the sand dunes near sunset brings you to scenic Wharariki Beach with its eroded rock stacks just off shore. A morning coffee on the shores of Lake Rotoroa in Nelson Lakes National Park is a great way to start off the day.

Wharariki Beach near Farewell Spit.

⁄ *Lush rainforest near the summit of the Mt Stokes Track, Marlborough Sounds.*

A misty morning along the Motueka River.

Swans at Lake Rotoroa, Nelson Lakes National Park.

Kayaks on Onetahuti Beach, Abel Tasman National Park.

◁ Titirangi Bay from Grant Lookout.

49

West Coast

From the blowholes at the unusually layered Pancake Rocks to the milky blue glacial rivers flowing down from the Southern Alps, the West Coast boasts incredible and dramatic variety. A hike or flight over the glaciers at Fox or Franz Josef is well worth the trouble it takes to get there. Those willing to rise before dawn can enjoy the reflection of the mountains in mirror-still Lake Matheson; pre-dawn is the best time of day to take advantage of the view.

Peter's Pool near Fox Glacier, Westland National Park.

⬑ Whanganui River, near Harihari, Westland.

Little Grey River, near Reefton.

⬅ *Blowhole at the Pancake Rocks, Punakaiki, Papanui National Park.*

The classic morning view of the Southern Alps from Lake Matheson.

Fox Glacier, Westland.

Canterbury

One of my favourite places in all of New Zealand is the south end of the brilliant, turquoise blue Lake Pukaki. You can pull your campervan right up to the edge of the lake and watch the sun set with Mount Cook visible at the far shore. A strenuous walk up to Red Tarns in the late afternoon gives access to a collection of small mountain tarns that offer the summit of snow-covered Mount Cook as backdrop.

The summit of Mt Cook/Aoraki as viewed from a helicopter.

Fisherman on Lake Ruataniwha near Twizel.

Autumn colours near the town of Twizel.

↳ Red Tarns with Mt Cook in the background.

Lupins blooming near Lake Tekapo.

The Seaward Kaikoura Range from Point Kean.

Akaroa Harbour, Banks Peninsula.

Waimakariri Valley, Arthur's Pass National Park.

Otago

Stretching from the Otago Peninsula near Dunedin to the heights of Mount Aspiring National Park to the west of Wanaka, the Otago region is certainly worth a visit. For me, hiking in the backcountry of Mount Aspiring National Park is the area's real gem. Experiencing the view down the West Matukituki Valley from French Ridge framed by a rainbow made the 900m scramble worth every difficult step.

Lake Wakatipu from Skyline Lookout, Queenstown.

Rob Roy Valley, Mt Aspiring National Park.

65

The iconic Moeraki Boulders at sunrise.

Orchard in autumn, Cromwell.

67

Rough seas at Nugget Point in the Catlins.

Rolling green hills and a morning rainbow in the Dart River Valley near Glenorchy.

The Dunedin Railway Station, Dunedin.

Harris Range from Treble Cone, Wanaka.

West Matukituki River, Mt Aspiring National Park.

◊ Tramper on French Ridge track, Mt Aspiring National Park.

Fiordland & Southland

For me, Fiordland is all about the National Park of the same name and the spectacular glacier-carved fiords and valleys that define the landscape there. While Milford Sound is the best known and most accessible of the fiords, for the more intrepid, an overnight kayak trip on secluded and quiet Doubtful Sound is a hard experience to top.

Doubtful Sound, Fiordland National Park.

The Hollyford River.

Eglinton Valley, Fiordland National Park.

Milford Sound with Mitre Peak to the left, Fiordland National Park.

High tide in Doubtful Sound, Fiordland National Park.

Waterfall on Falls Creek next to the Milford Road, Fiordland National Park.

Published by
Hema Maps NZ Ltd
PO Box 58924 Botany
Auckland 2041 New Zealand
Ph: +64 9 273 6459
Fax: +64 9 273 6479
sales@hemamaps.co.nz
www.hemamaps.com

1st edition – 2010
ISBN: 978-1-87730-277-0

Copyright
© Hema Maps Pty Ltd 2010
Photographs
© Jeff Drewitz 2010

Publisher: Rob Boegheim
Cartographic Publishing Manager: Gavin James
Art Director: Natasha Muratidis
Author & Photographer: Jeff Drewitz
Editor: Natalie Wilson
Editorial Assistant & Project Leader: Kate Armstrong
Printing: Printed in Singapore by Tien Wah Press

Cover photograph: Trampers on trail to Mueller Hut,
Mt Cook/Aoraki National Park, South Island

\ *Sunrise over Lake Pukaki.*